Secondly~Finally

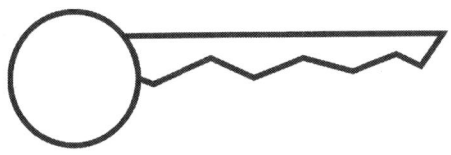

MICHAEL LEE

ORGANIC WEAPON ARTS
DETROIT, MI

Organic Weapon Arts Chapbook Series
Series Editors: Tarfia Faizullah & Jamaal May

Secondly. Finally
Copyright © 2015 by **Michael Lee** All rights reserved.
Printed in the United States of America

First Edition, 2015
ISBN: 978-0-9962585-0-0

Cover art by Jamaal May
Book layout by Jamaal May
Edited by Tarfia Faizullah

More from OW! Arts:
www.organicweaponarts.com

CONTENTS

I.

The Pill / 3
In One Story / 4
Sound Lost in the North / 6
The Law of Halves as Applied to the Blade / 7
Grindstone / 9
Fire / 10
The Taking of Lead / 12
Refraction / 15
The Blade as Key / 17

II.

The Survival of What Remains / 20
Self-Erasure as Applied to My Memory / 21
Alighted Clock / 26
Just Yesterday / 28
Secondly. Finally / 30
Glomma / 31

For Stephen
  Rest Well Little Brother

THE PILL

a small moon, or bomb,
which kills no one

quickly, dissolves the way a moment does,
over time and never

completely. The pill is a tooth of light
broken off the moon, enters the body

a blinding seed, tears open the dark
of me, hot lash of lightning splitting

the sky, a zipper across a black bag.
The pill is infinite, a solar system

in the blind man's eye. It is
a white shadow dragging night behind it

like a corpse. I've reached so far into the medicine
cabinet, my hand came back through my mouth.

I've looked into the mirror for so long,
I forgot what it was. I introduced myself,

tried to say my name and instead
my fist swung like a curse and broke

the glass. I knew I was gone
when I was knocked out by my own name.

Couldn't have told the cops what it looked like
if they asked me. "Came out of nowhere," I'd say.

"Took itself, and everything
I owned. Just left me here."

IN ONE STORY

one that isn't true, when I first hear
about your murder, I am in my backyard hunting—
not the birds, but the sounds they make.

An arrow, like a curse, is silent after it leaves
the mouth of a bow, then only a thrumming is left
as it coils through the hands. What better way

to pierce any music than with silence?
The knife too would have been silent. I picture
you as a song now, because its easier

to remember you that way, after all
these years, than to picture each tooth
of your smile, removed by time, like a note struck

dead. And when it ends, the song
rather than your life, it is always less final—
as though it might begin again—

less final than your headstone,
less final than your windbreaker which hangs
now in my closet and the 67 cents

in the front pocket, which will never be spent.
In this way I never actually killed a bird, just their songs.
Though, it could be argued, without its song

is a bird even alive? I cleaned and skinned
each rhythm and packaged them away
in the cellar. It was the middle of Winter

and beginning that day it would always be
the middle of Winter. We must stay warm,
somehow. I collected all the birds, their mouths

moving silently like half working gadgets. I carried them
up the telephone pole, placing each along the wire
and from their mouths came hundreds of voices, then thousands

saying only your name and your mother's name and the word *knife*,
knife, so many times the knife grew infinite, and then your age
was repeated so many times until you too, thirteen, would live forever.

SOUND LOST IN THE NORTH

And there, the light clank and moan
of the wind chimes spread out across the garden.
An unexplained crack in a windshield. Frost
across a pane of glass, you could watch it

all at once. Minnesota winter is like that:
far enough north and you have to strain to hear
a distant rifle, especially if it finds its mark—the sound
disappears with the bullet, into the meat.

That's when you might imagine following the sound of the gun
and living in that moment—where the body, of whatever it was,
swallows the bullet along with its sound. Imagine
what that would to do to the sap or the blood.

My grandfather was a craftsman
and either he spoke of it or I dreamt of a hammer
in his left atrium. The winter was so thick,
when he died the sound had nowhere to go
and so I saw him follow a faint tinkering
down and into his own body.

I've known nights so cold the body is unlikely to bleed.
In a miracle, the shot might awaken the heart,
like a kick to an engine shaking the frost out
of its pistons, but even that would be lost

among the snow. I have braved my own heart and swung
a hammer so honestly that smoke curled off the nail.
Still there was no sound. In my grandfather's name
I have hefted an axe in the dead of winter,
but still there was no sound, not even enough to follow

down into the wood. Each moment of winter is so faint
and silent it is a memory even as you live it. And so it was
then, as the hammer fell with such repetition it became slow and soft
falling downward like snow, again and again, until the birds froze mid-song.
And the wordless chimes swayed like dark ropes.

THE LAW OF HALVES AS APPLIED TO THE BLADE

2.
The news said it had been done with a kitchen knife,
it had been done fifteen times. Earlier that day
my math teacher had stepped towards the blackboard
proving that if you continue to halve a distance
between two points you will never reach the end.

1.
The next morning I stood two feet from the door.
Then one foot. Then six inches. Eventually,
with only centimeters remaining I gave up, deterred
by the endless impossibility of getting through the day.

.5
From the onset of forward motion, the knife
must have been two feet from the first point of entry.
I picture it then being one foot. Then six inches.

.25
Imagining the rule of halves applied to the blade
its point still hovers over his chest. His shirt
is clean and his hair dry, and I have grown older
waiting for him to return. The knife
is barely moving now, ten years later,
like a shiny metal train creeping into the chest
of a station where everyone is dressed in red.

.125
He has had time to ask his mother why
she is pointing a knife at him. She has had time
to notice his new haircut, the way his eyes are wet
and catch the glint of the sun bathed blade.
She has had time to notice his clean shirt,
which she would remember as having had been red.

.0625
The passengers never imagined when the train entered,
then left, that they would slide back in. And out. And
in fifteen times like a sewing machine undoing a shirt.

0.
At the onset of forward
motion his shirt was white.

GRINDSTONE

I found the grindstone in the cellar last week.
I sharpened every blade we had. Come dusk
the hatchet was last, the glint of it a wet fang.
To sharpen a dulled axe-head is to undress
the last of the farm fed to the new machines.
It is the antithesis of the tomb. The tenor of the stone is
singed and howling. I fed it, like a trapped wolf,
rusted husk after husk until the last hilt
writhed in my hand. I swung the thing like a reckless grin
and punctured the whole month. A sterling rain spilled
from the gut of it. The last day of July,
thick as a dead boy's name caught in the throat,
bloody as a mouth brimming with a fist-
full of silvered teeth. The sun dimmed,
a gaunt glow of steel slowly darkening.

FIRE

I sat by the fire, gave it newspaper
after paper, headlines

turning to smoke within
the wall's ossuary, set deep like an eye

spun dark by hunger, a stone mouth
weaving stories to light.

O' deft apprentice of devouring.
O' draftsmen of thinning, journeyman

of the spindle made by the small gods
of burning, I've seen the flames shuck loose

the proof that today even happened.
I've spent whole Sundays erasing

whole Sundays as the flames make
erasures of their own shadows

cast violently against the brick. Let me hide,
too, these pages here beneath the garb

of smoke, and the fire hissing
out of the pine and birch, dashing

so quickly its almost as if it had lived
here in the wood all along. A civilization

of gilt heat released by flint, and stave,
dressed in sulfur and spark.

Village of light fleeing through the dark throat
of the chimney to vanish, as if vanishing

were a type of freedom. This paper,
a key when lit—

strange how a story, then, is the key
to its own undoing, similarly

the body. This story of fire
winging out of the wood
best explains myself to me,
the ways in which I am afraid of my own hands,

the ways in which I have unlocked another man's jaw,
and my own blood from my skin. The way I sparked

the pipe, like a trumpet which fires music back
into the mouth, and the smoke exited

in a rustle of grey wings.
As if it had lived in me all along

and took me with it as it went,
one small bone at a time.

THE TAKING OF LEAD

1.
There are more color receptors in the human eye
than are used. The colors of the world as they are seen
are not the true colors. The true colors have no names

and so they are impossible to imagine. The failure of language
is not that something can only be described with a limited number
of words, but that it can only be perceived using those words.

2.
Holding his fingers to the light the man said to his son,
"this hand is good for breaking, for building, the hand is
a machine. Now, imagine you do not know the hand's name,
tell me then, what is it not capable of?"

3.
The occurrence of war outside the boy's window
was as frequent as the birds. Each night,
he watched from behind the blinds

as soldiers emerged from the thicket
smooth and quiet as apparitions or memories
climbing down from the skull and into the tall grass.

The steel rods they carried burst with sparks
and tore each other down at the neck and knees.
His father told him these were the inventions

of lesser minds, demented by baseness and old magic.
These burning branches could swallow the stare
of a man and drive him straight into the ground.

It was a time when guns were not discussed
by name, or even during day, only by description
and behind locked doors where it was believed

they could not enter. To the boy and his father,
the nameless machines were capable of anything.
They did not understand why they were only used to kill.

4.
The boy knew nothing but the bodies next to the garden,
the crows discussing the rites of flesh. In the morning
he would wade dizzily through the pints of men. One by one

with a silver spoon he would remove the lead
musket balls from the skulls and chests and legs of the dead men
and carry them to his father to be melted down and turned to gold.

When the man was finished, he would bring a vat
of burning gold back to the field and pour a spoonful
into each of the wounds from which the lead was taken.

Time and time again the boy watched the bodies
as their eyes rolled back from the depths of the skull,
shine in the waning light of day like lanterns along a river.

The soldiers would rise as fog does. In silence,
they would empty the grass and return to the forest.
Come nightfall they would re-emerge to kill each other again.
Automatons clad in blood.

5.
Everyday the boy asked his father why
he would reawake the soldiers, and each time
his father said,

"After a war, the side with the most land and least dead
dances and makes love inside the sound of drums.
It seems to me, this is all the body has ever wanted.

"I wish to see if there will ever come a time when,
upon reawakening, they will each forget their language
and not know the name for the those terrible burning snouts

"they carry. These are dangerous men—not because
they carry a weapon, but because what they carry is named
and so it has only one imaginable purpose.

"Imagine, the whole field of soldiers forgetting their language
and being possessed only by what their bodies want most in the end:

to dance, and to love. I wonder if we would see the field break

"into a brilliant cavorting, the branches firing upwards, and those steel rods peeling back the dark cowl of night. How everything would be illuminated like cathedrals, empty of language, and teeming with sound."

REFRACTION

I have come to believe death is a relationship
between two objects. Though, perhaps it is more
like a message or sudden idea. For instance,

the blade meets the body for the first time, they strike
up a conversation. Death steps from each of their mouths
and then rises in an aggregate of shadows between them.

Or the blade, like a letter, carries the notion,
which the body has never even considered. The knife
does not kill the body, it simply informs it that death is possible,

a sudden light flooding the room,
mortality is illuminated inside of us, the one corner
of the house we never knew to exist

until all other rooms had darkened. Once, I saw myself
in a storefront window and felt lost somewhere in the middle,
a single word stuck between two people. I stared at my reflection

and wondered if dying would be as simple as shattering
a window. Once, I couldn't find myself in a house
of mirrors, by which I mean I was everywhere.

I knelt beside the lake and drank
the water for I was in it. I threw a stone
through the shop window for I was in it.

When my mouth grew dry, I fed myself the knife,
as though it were a second tongue, for I was in it.
These are the ways the body misinterprets thirst.

I knew a man who drank himself
to death. It was not the alcohol that killed him,
it was his reflection which never left the glass,

not even as it fell and the whiskey carried him
across the floor, refracting again and again
into the dark of the window. We found death

is just a thinning. Scrubbing away a stain
on a shirt until the shirt itself is gone
and the hand moves in a circle as if cleaning the air.

THE BLADE AS KEY

Boy who was himself a door, fifteen
red keyholes appearing wherever

the key fell, the way a shovel is a key
to the earth, though the boy never opens

wide enough to walk through, just enough
to see into the infinite rooms lit with planets gazing

back out, boy with a locked galaxy inside of him.
The police asked why his blood was black,

why it shone and was riddled
with what looked to be stars, why his blood ran

from the house, and into the street
where it continued on to the sea,

lifted into the sky and then became it.
Now, there is a place in the Pacific

where it is always night.
His magnificent blood

is a wet universe gazing down on us.
His blood, an endless dream

lit by stars as it all runs
from the keyholes of his sternum, opening

like fifteen eyes which see
forever.

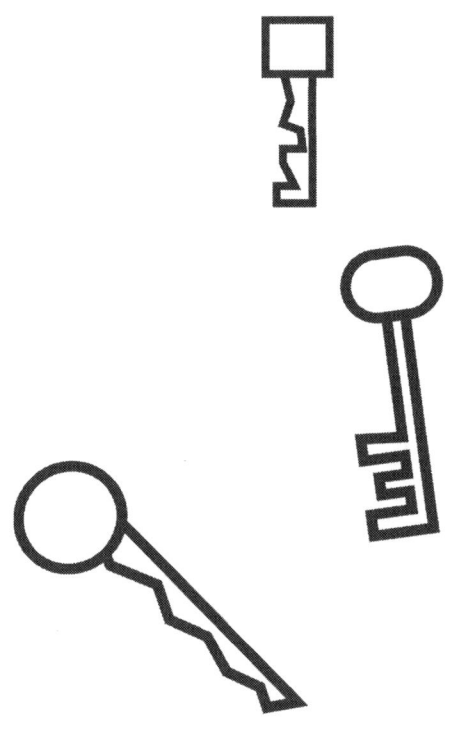

THE SURVIVAL OF WHAT REMAINS

In the desert, the heat itself is a thief
and steals rain from the body. The stone,
red as a bloodshot eye. The dawn
opens like a hinge. A single raven

bows from a fence post again and again
as we pass its mantra of rustling, its wings flaring
as if to welcome us into the blackness
of its endless mouth. Its unimaginable eyes.
How easy it would be to give myself away to this

small hunger, this fist sized silhouette opening its body
like a mangled hand. Imagine the heart,
so thick with blood it must seem black
as a raven, imagine how it might look if it were to unfurl

in exhaustion, something like a burnt map
across a table, a black thing with wings. Imagine the span
of the wings, thus the span of love and of survival,
which eventually begin to mean the same thing
until it is clear that they always have.

There is a pulse even in stone and in the sleeping corpses
of cattle strewn across the clay lips of the horizon, deflated
almost entirely of life save a distant tick, like that of a clock,
in their sharpened bones digging out from their hide, as if to escape.

I have seen death sharpen its beak on the dry air and life climb out
of a starved thing to then become wind. If the bone and the breath
can survive the body then the body can survive these long days
where the sun sets like a guillotine and the heart opens
as though it could fly clean out of the mouth.

SELF ERASURE AS APPLIED TO MY MEMORY

24.
It was the season of ghosts locked
in the windowpanes and the cellar lamp,
the grindstone abandoned amongst the coal, generation
after generation, it was the year the abandoned house
down the block burned to the ground, and then another
fell into itself and both sprouted into strange mansions
with ghostless windows and storyless attics. My grandmother
became the bedsheets, though thinner than
the bedsheets, until she vanished like the words
'I love you', just hours after I last said them.
Sometimes I believe I had, in a way,
given her permission to go, my ego tells me this.
It was the year the ego grew legs and made
things tumble and burn. It was the year
I didn't sleep, but could not leave my bed.
It was the year of vanishing
which I had learned from the dead.
It was the year I became the pipe,
then the couch, and then the air as it whistled
through my bones like a bolt. It was the year
I did not eat unless it was moonlight or blue
light of the television. It was the year
I did not dream and spoke only in curses.
It was the year magic fell dead in the street
like a struck crow, and darkened beneath
the cars as they left, and kept leaving.
That year my friend was murdered, and though
I can remember his laugh, and his hair-
how it came to a widows peak, his afro
a kind of curled crown-I recall nothing else, not his eyes
or his body, and now, barely his smile. That year,
my grandfather, too, died, I can remember
him shaving, but I cannot recall his face
or the hair that must have been there.
That year the crops, which had not been grown on our land
for a hundred years, came up through the floorboards,
and from the faucets, and all of our mouths were full
of grain, and corn, and drought, and shadows. It was the year

I lived on a train and passed the rusted ship yards
outside of New York heading into Connecticut. The train burned
and burned like a whistle and drove straight
into the sea. That year, from the windows which I guarded
like a ghost, I watched someone else's grandfather feeding
his cat on the countryside, the man gazed out into the horizon
as though he noticed, just then, half his life was missing
from his memory. I am told that it too was the year
I was dying, I would sleep on the kitchen floor
after each meal, a plug of tobacco tucked gently into my lip
as though it were a thing that could wake or wake something in me.
Some dream seed rupturing in the mouth. I don't remember
this, it is a false memory, it is the image of the Mona Lisa
as described to you by the janitor of the Louvre,
and though he or she knows the painting best-the coy look
of mischief, the conquering nature of the eyes-
without seeing it that image is not yours, or even mine,
just as each story that has ever been told is hardly a replica
of light. It was the year I remembered and remembered
and remembered as if the act of remembering was like sharpening
a blade until the blade was gone. Only a hilt, now. Only nothing.
It was the year when I was twenty-four or maybe twelve
but probably six, it was the year in which all years became the same,
and my whole life existed in a single moment, one dream
fading away, a block of salt worn by rain, drop by drop.

12.
It was the season of ghosts
in the wind   and
                  abandoned   coal, generation
after generation,   the   house
                burned to the ground
fell into itself and   sprouted   strange
     ghostless windows a   storyless attic . My grandmother
became   thinner than
                            the words

                 I had
given her   my ego tells me
It was the year the ego   made
things   burn. It was the year
I didn't   leave my bed.

It was the year of vanishing,

    the year I became the pipe,
        then the air as it whistled
through   the year
I did not eat
        It was the year
I did not dream and spoke only in curses.
    magic fell dead in the street
    and darkened
    and kept leaving.
That year my friend was murdered,
    his laugh,
        his afro
a   curled crown, I recall nothing else,
        That year,
my grandfather   died
  shaving, but i cannot recall his face
    that must have been there.
That year
  a hundred years came
    from the faucets, and all of our mouths were full
of   drought and shadows. It was the year
I lived   in   the rusted ship yards
outside of New York
and burned like a whistle   straight
into the sea   which I guarded
like a ghost,   someone else's grandfather fe d
            the horizon

  his memory.   that   year
I was dying, I would sleep on the   floor
    a plug of tobacco tucked   in   my lip
as though it were a thing that could wake
· Some dream   rupturing in the mouth

  described   by the janitor of   Lo v e,
and
of mischief,
       it   is not yours, or   mine,
   each story   is hardly
  light

```
                    the act of remembering      like sharpening
a blade
It was the year when I was            or maybe
but probably      it was the year in which all years became the same,
and my whole life existed in a single               dream
                    worn by rain


6.
It was the season of ghost
      wind
              and                      coal
                        the              house
                 burned to the ground
              and      sprouted
                         storyless


                              words




I didn't
          vanish

          I became the pipe,
              then the air

I did not eat
                       the
           dream        only    curses
                       dead
                       dark
                       and      leaving.
That year              was murdered,




                              That year
```

                        came
     from the faucets,

and burned

like

Some dream   rupturing   the mouth.

ALIGHTED CLOCK

Let the coffee remain lukewarm forever.
Let the fan blade rest, not like the feather

of a slain bird, but the knife which lives
in its side, and the hours

that placed it there, those same hours
which displace the organs of the body, moved

inside my grandfather until there was no room
for him inside of himself, and so he left, lives now

in the shadows as they pass across the afternoon
like the ceremony of traffic

devoured by dusk, a flock of geese
migrating in silence. Some of him now lives

in the exhaust of the Blandin Paper Mill
along the rapids, the buzz of power-

lines rattled by the softness of snow,
in which he also lives, and in the clock—

which tells us nothing
we didn't already know—

behind the counter of this cafe,
as the shop empties onto the sidewalk like a libation

for all these years now inside of me,
and the parts of me they have removed. As I turn
from the window and from the traffic and the rain outside,
I imagine I have always been here and will never be

anywhere else, and the liquor store and pharmacy
across the street are worlds away, maybe

even invented memories; almost like you, woman I love,

seem to be now, 1,000 miles away.

Once you told me, "We ourselves are time",
and when you called just hours ago

to say you are not pregnant, I don't imagine
that you could hear how I did not smile,

though we are young and unprepared,
for I knew then, what I always knew,

that you would leave me,
because when I came inside you, for the last time,

I became you entirely, and so, by necessity,
left myself and showed you how to go.

Just as time does and has always done,
like a long rope of breath leaving the body as if leading us

out of ourselves. Time teaches us nothing we didn't already know,
to leave and keep leaving. I don't know if love should feel

this way, like something that inhabits the body
and pushes it out of itself, but here I go

across the slick streets at night,
these interstates darkened by thought

as the median paint runs together
into one white line like the hem of an elegant gown.

JUST YESTERDAY

Your pain, or any pain, isn't worth any more than the words
    we can dig up to describe it.
            Tell me of the knife,
                  but make it pretty.
Tell me of the collar bone
    reaching out of the skin like a branch,
                but make it soft.
Everyone wants us to spill
        poetically, in a way
            that goes down easy,
they want us speak of maps
        by referring to their borders
and not by what's inside of them.   I dreamt you still
                      named.
I dreamt you naked. I dreamt you leaking
        from the knife's advances,
            I dreamt you siphoning out your own life
through the needle,
    I dreamt your spine crumbling
        like a palace of cards,
I dreamt every dead person I know
        was the same and lived
            in the same cramped ally of my skull.
I'll tell you these stories until the words materialize
            and I can stop   up a wound,
I know,   I might as well try to gather the rain with a sieve,
    but goddammit I need to try.
        I've been walking around believing the dead
are like windows, this poem and other poems
        a hand full of rocks, I want to shatter
            each of your faces, O' family,
O' friends, like you
    might walk out from behind those gaps
        in your smiles. Sometimes, I hold a word
to my ear like a conch shell. Sometimes I curse
        the ocean for what it cannot or will not say.
I surround these bodies
    with sentence after sentence
        and the words chant like a crowd,

the words become music,
        the words become an orchestra of flies.
                I almost believe you will wake up, all of you,
together. I almost believe your name
                will slither
                      its way back into your body
and you will kick back to life like a junkyard Cutlass
and you will walk out of your own funerals
                laughing. How absurd,
                    this choir of weeping,
these caskets planted in the dirt like seeds.
       It is so cold in this Winter's lexicon, this language
                of nothing, of once was or never will be
again, sometimes I want to kill
        my uncle for being a more miserable drunk than I
            was. Sometimes I want him to die already so I can
write about it, sometimes
        I too want to be a poem.
            I don't want to be this pain, but the language
used to unearth it. Sometimes, I curse archeologists
       for their basic tools telling us basic things.
                Sometimes, I think scientists are lazy
I too could dig a heart out of a chest.
        What do any of them know about pulling
            the history out of a body, without killing it?
Just yesterday, scientists discovered a new ligament
       in the human knee. Just yesterday I found out
        I can't sleep for a whole new set of reasons.
Just yesterday I wrote and wrote and wrote and kept
       writing, because I've committed to not killing
                anyone, especially myself.
Just yesterday
       I found new ways to say I miss you, my god
                how I miss you all.

SECONDLY. FINALLY

Who tells your story now, heaven faced
boy? Sometimes I fear I may have killed you

a second time, how silence is a kind of death, how
having your story told for you

is also a kind of death, and journalists
then are well educated, and studious

assassins. Secondly, or finally,
I continue to begin with the end

as if that's all there is, as if you were
birthed here by the knife, bled into

the world through your own wounds.
Some days I feel I have taken on your shadow

and am the appropriator of your aunt's
grief, which is dull and silent

like a round stone in the shoe
as it works its way into the skin and will

eventually, through the blood, become
a part of the body, a knob or handle in the bone

as if this grief could open us,
a skeleton, a screen door

a bolt of silk
unraveling. My memory

of you cinches tight and I tell the story
from the beginning, this time

you are alive, this time
I say nothing.

GLOMMA

The canoe cut through the river,
a single bolt of black lightning

opening an even more thorough darkness,
a comb sliding through the hair, a tangled memory

released. White cows, horned and thundering,
stumbled along the bank like sculptures of moonlight

moving through the tall brush to drink
their own shimmering faces. Night fell

around the valley, and one by one
the orange lights of the farm houses turned

on so slowly behind the windows, opening
in their glow, it seemed as though each house

woke up to gaze out onto the river,
past the canoe and our silence, past the cattle

and their bells ringing, those same bells
which have been ringing for a hundred years,

the same song passed from animal to animal
in a shared history. Each bell carries a different note

and if even one animal is slain, or lost,
the entire composition is undone.

This is how I understand music,
the way it is given to the next

generation again and again, the bells
a constant music of the country, so steady

and familiar, the entire village came to believe
that it is the stars that are ringing

as they open, thousands of small windows
into an endless morning, that morning which is always

tomorrow, past the one tractor still rumbling across the dark field,
racing the first frost stirring somewhere just beyond the pines

and the mining town with no mine now,
where the soul opens and one person stares out

of another, beyond their frame and clouds passing
inside them, so quietly only the shadows make sound

as they move darkly across the grass.
No, to see through someone

is not an insult, it is to say you contain worlds,
whole landscapes past the breathing sill of the body.

ACKNOWLEDGEMENTS

I would like to thank all who assisted me in bringing these poems and this book into the world. A special thanks to the Minnesota State Arts Board and the Metropolitan Regional Arts Council for allowing me the time and space to craft many of these poems. To the beautiful folks at Organic Weapon, and of course my brother Jeremiah Bey who has played a monumental role in my personal and artistic journey.

Grateful acknowledgements are due to the editors of the journals where some of these poems first appeared:

Grindstone: Indiana Review
The Taking of Lead: Rattle
Sound Lost in the North: Prime Number
Law of Halves as Applied to the Blade: Phoebe
The Survival of What Remains: Phoebe
The Pill: Carolina Quarterly
Self-Erasure as Applied to My Memory: Carolina Quarterly
The Blade as Key: Ninth Letter
Secondly. Finally: Ninth Letter